recommended standards for teacher education

the accreditation of basic and advanced preparation programs for professional school personnel

Prepared by the
Evaluative Criteria
Study Committee
and adopted by the
Executive Committee
of AACTE
for transmittal to the
National Council
for Accreditation
of Teacher Education

November 1969

The American Association of Colleges for Teacher Education
One Dupont Circle, Washington, D.C. 20036

This report includes the results of pilot-testing an earlier draft of these standards which was done pursuant to Contract No. OEC-3-8-080248-0030(010) with the U.S. Department of Health, Education, and Welfare, Office of Education.

Published 1969 by the
AMERICAN ASSOCIATION OF COLLEGES FOR TEACHER EDUCATION
One Dupont Circle, Washington, D. C. 20036

Standard Book Number 910052-41-7
Library of Congress Catalog Number 74-107867

Contents

LB
1715
A622

Foreword
Introduction

Part I: Basic Teacher Education Programs

PROGRAMS FOR THE INITIAL PREPARATION OF TEACHERS THROUGH THE FIFTH-YEAR LEVEL, INCLUDING M.A.T. PROGRAMS

1. Curricula for Basic Programs

1.1 Design of Curricula	3
1.2 The General Studies Component	3
1.3 The Professional Studies Component	4
1.3.1 Content for the Teaching Specialty	4
1.3.2 Humanistic and Behavioral Studies	5
1.3.3 Teaching and Learning Theory With Laboratory and Clinical Experience	5
1.3.4 Practicum	6
1.4 Use of Guidelines Developed by National Learned Societies and Professional Associations	6
1.5 Control of Basic Programs	7

2. Faculty for Basic Programs

2.1 Competence and Utilization of Faculty	7
2.2 Faculty Involvement with Schools	8
2.3 Conditions for Faculty Service	8
2.4 Part-time Faculty	9

3. Students in Basic Programs

3.1 Admission to Basic Programs	9
3.2 Retention of Students in Basic Programs	10
3.3 Counseling and Advising for Students in Basic Programs	10
3.4 Student Participation in Program Evaluation and Development	10

4. Resources and Facilities for Basic Programs

4.1 Library	11
4.2 Materials and Instructional Media Center	11
4.3 Physical Facilities and Other Resources	12

5. Evaluation, Program Review, and Planning

5.1 Evaluation of Graduates	12
5.2 Use of Evaluation Results to Improve Basic Programs	12
5.3 Long-Range Planning	13

Part II: Advanced Programs

POST-BACCALAUREATE PROGRAMS FOR THE ADVANCED PREPARATION OF TEACHERS AND THE PREPARATION OF OTHER PROFESSIONAL SCHOOL PERSONNEL

G-1. Curricula for Advanced Programs

G-1.1 Design of Curricula	14
G-1.2 Content of Curricula	14
G-1.3 Research in Advanced Curricula	15
G-1.4 Individualization of Programs of Study	15
G-1.5 Use of Guidelines Developed by National Learned Societies and Professional Associations	16
G-1.6 Quality Controls	16
G-1.6.1 Graduate Credit	16
G-1.6.2 Graduate Level Courses	16
G-1.6.3 Residence Study	16
G-1.7 Control of Advanced Programs	17

G-2. Faculty for Advanced Programs

G-2.1 Preparation of Faculty	17
G-2.2 Composition of Faculty for Doctoral Degree Programs	18
G-2.3 Conditions for Faculty Service	18
G-2.4 Part-time Faculty	19

G-3. Students in Advanced Programs

G-3.1 Admission to Advanced Programs	19
G-3.2 Retention of Students in Advanced Programs	20
G-3.3 Planning and Supervision of Students' Programs of Study	20
G-3.4 Student Participation in Program Evaluation and Development	20

G-4. Resources and Facilities for Advanced Programs

G-4.1 Library	21
G-4.2 Physical Facilities and Other Resources	21

G-5. Evaluation, Program Review, and Planning

G-5.1 Evaluation of Graduates	21
G-5.2 Use of Evaluation Results to Improve Advanced Programs	22
G-5.3 Long-Range Planning	22

Foreword

These recommended standards for teacher education are the culmination of an intensive three-year study sponsored by the American Association of Colleges for Teacher Education under the leadership of its Evaluative Criteria Study Committee. They represent another step in the unending process to improve the accreditation of teacher education. While developed primarily for accreditation purposes, they may also be viewed as general guidelines for the improvement of preparation programs for professional school personnel.

These standards are recommended by the AACTE Executive Committee to the National Council for Accreditation of Teacher Education for adoption and implementation. The AACTE submits these recommendations in response to its mandate from the National Commission on Accrediting as put forth in the NCATE constitution to continuously evaluate and revise the accreditation standards.

In transmitting new standards to NCATE, the Association acknowledges that they are not, and should not be, the final word in standards for accrediting teacher education. It recognizes that standards must be systematically reviewed and revised in terms of experience in using them, in light of societal changes, and in relation to advances in the state of the art of educating professional school personnel. The AACTE takes seriously its assigned responsibility and is committed to provide leadership for the continuous evaluation and revision of these standards.

The pattern of involvement which has characterized the development of these new standards is envisioned as a guide for evaluating and revising them in the future. Representatives of colleges and universities engaged in teacher education, learned societies and professional associations, state departments of education, and of the teaching profession have participated in the development of these recommendations. The Committee has conducted an opinion survey of the present NCATE standards, prepared and distributed resource materials, and has sponsored regional conferences to discuss relevant issues and to collect ideas for improving standards. It has written preliminary drafts, submitted them to the field for reaction, and revised them accordingly. In cooperation with NCATE and under a contract with the Bureau of Research of the United States Office of Education, the Committee has tested the feasibility of the proposed new standards in eight colleges and universities, and has further revised its proposals in light of the test results. Through intense and protracted effort, the Committee has endeavored to maintain a unified rationale for standards while reconciling many and different points of view submitted by participants in the study.

The AACTE wishes to express its appreciation to the many persons, institutions, and agencies for their many contributions of time and resources without which these standards could not have been developed. In the final analysis, the indirect results of the process utilized in this study may be as significant as the standards themselves. In support of this process, the financial assistance of the ESSO Education Foundation and the U. S. Steel Foundation supplemented in a significant way the funding provided by the Association and its member institutions.

The quality of these recommended standards has been made possible by the insightful views concerning teacher education contributed by members of the Evaluative Criteria Study Committee. Special words of commendation are presented to the National Council for Accreditation of Teacher Education and its director, Rolf Larson, for their cooperation and assistance during the Feasibility Project; to Edwin P. Adkins and Paul F. Sharp, Chairman and Vice Chairman of the Committee, for their untiring leadership; and to Karl Massanari for the total commitment of his many talents to the success of this venture. Members of the Committee and staff are identified on the following page.

EDWARD C. POMEROY
Executive Secretary, AACTE

November, 1969

Evaluative Criteria Study Committee

Chairman—Edwin P. Adkins, Associate Vice President, Temple University, Philadelphia, Pennsylvania

Vice Chairman—Paul F. Sharp, President, Drake University, Des Moines, Iowa

Harry S. Broudy, Professor of Philosophy of Education, University of Illinois, Urbana, Illinois

Robert N. Bush, Professor of Education, Stanford University, Stanford, California

Margaret Knispel, Assistant Secretary, National Commission on Teacher Education and Professional Standards, Washington, D. C.

Margaret Lindsey, Professor of Education, Teachers College, Columbia University, New York

Warren C. Lovinger, President, Central Missouri State College, Warrensburg, Missouri

Robert MacVicar, Chancellor, Southern Illinois University, Carbondale, Illinois

Sister Mary Emil, Director of Educational Research, Marygrove College, Detroit, Michigan

E. C. Merrill, President, Gallaudet College, Washington, D. C.

Harold Shane, University Professor of Education, Indiana University, Bloomington, Indiana

Kimball Wiles, Dean, College of Education, University of Florida, Gainesville, Florida

(Dr. Wiles' untimely death in February 1968 brought to a close a term of service marked by distinction and dedication.)

Staff

Karl Massanari, Associate Secretary, AACTE, and Director of the AACTE/NCATE Feasibility Project

Richard L. James, Associate Secretary, AACTE, and Associate Director of the AACTE/NCATE Feasibility Project

Shirley Bonneville, Secretary, AACTE

Introduction

National accreditation of college and university programs for the preparation of all teachers and other professional school personnel at the elementary and secondary levels is the exclusive responsibility of the National Council for Accreditation of Teacher Education (NCATE). The NCATE has been authorized by the National Commission on Accrediting to adopt standards and procedures for accreditation and to determine the accreditation status of institutional programs for preparing teachers and other professional school personnel.

Purposes of National Accreditation of Teacher Education

National accreditation of teacher education serves four major purposes:

1. To assure the public that particular institutions—those named in the Annual List—offer programs for the preparation of teachers and other professional school personnel that meet national standards of quality
2. To ensure that children and youth are served by well-prepared school personnel
3. To advance the teaching profession through the improvement of preparation programs
4. To provide a practical basis for reciprocity among the states in certifying professional school personnel.

Institutional Self-Governance and National Accreditation

Both public and private institutions of higher learning in the United States have a long heritage of self-governance. The right of colleges and universities to set their own goals and to shape their own destinies has accounted for a large measure of the excellence—perhaps inadequacy as well—which is found among institutions of higher learning today. The freedom of institutions to move toward higher levels of excellence should be encouraged and supported by national accreditation. When accreditation distracts an institution from this mission, or encroaches upon its freedom to accomplish it, the accreditation process becomes incompatible with its own purposes.

It is equally true, however, that national accreditation can exert a countervailing force when institutions aspire to expand programs beyond the capacity of available resources and when they offer marginal or poor programs. National accreditation represents a common floor of acceptability. Each institution of higher learning is free to seek or not to seek national accreditation.

National Standards for Accreditation of Teacher Education

Accreditation by the National Council for Accreditation of Teacher Education certifies that the institution's programs for preparing teachers and other professional school personnel meet the standards. The institution is expected to meet the standards at a level judged acceptable at the time of its evaluation. However, in a profession where the state of the art is constantly improving, the level should be expected to rise. NCATE accreditation validates the quality of preparation programs and signifies that persons recommended by the institution can be expected to perform satisfactorily in typical teaching and other professional school positions throughout the United States. While the standards which are applied to programs are "minimum standards" for acceptability, the NCATE urges institutions to set higher standards for themselves and to strive for better ways to prepare teachers and other professional school personnel.

Continuous Review of NCATE Standards

The Constitution of the National Council for Accreditation of Teacher Education (Article VII, Section B) states:

> Responsibility for carrying on a systematic program of evaluation of standards and development of new and revised standards shall be allocated to the AACTE. The AACTE shall ensure the participation of representatives of institutions, organizations and fields of study concerned with teacher education, and the Council. The AACTE shall receive and consider recommendations about existing or revised standards from institutions which prepare teachers and from individuals and organizations concerned with teacher education.

The AACTE is carrying out this responsibility with maximum participation of those persons and organizations most directly concerned with accreditation standards.

The NCATE is committed to the proposition that its standards should reflect changing conditions in higher education generally and in teacher education in particular. This means that the standards will not remain static nor be pegged to any level of excellence, and that, from time to time, the floor of acceptability will be raised.

Applicability of NCATE Standards

The NCATE standards are divided into two parts: Part I, Basic Programs and Part II, Advanced Programs. The standards in Part I are to be applied to all *basic* programs: programs for the initial preparation of teachers (nursery school through secondary school) including five-year and M.A.T. programs. They are not applicable to programs for the preparation of teacher aids or other paraprofessionals.

The standards in Part II are to be applied to all *advanced* programs: programs beyond the baccalaureate level and beyond the basic programs for the preparation of teachers and other professional school personnel. They are not applicable to programs for the preparation of college teachers.

The standards in both Part I and Part II apply to all institutional programs leading to degrees or certificates regardless of the location and time at which the instruction takes place.

Eligibility for NCATE Accreditation

Degree-granting institutions are eligible for an evaluation by NCATE if they offer programs for the preparation of teachers and/or other professional school personnel, are accredited by the appropriate regional accrediting association, and are approved by the appropriate state department of education at the levels and in the categories for which NCATE accreditation is sought. While an institution is expected to present for review *all* of its programs for the preparation of teachers and other professional school personnel, only those programs from which some students have been graduated are eligible for accreditation.

The Council regards accreditation by a regional accrediting association as reasonable assurance of the overall quality of an institution, including its general financial stability, the effectiveness of its administration, the adequacy of its general facilities, the quality of its student personnel program, the strength of its faculty, the adequacy of its faculty personnel policies, the conditions of faculty service, and the quality of instruction.

An institution accepted for evaluation shall present for review:

1. *All basic programs:* programs offered for the initial preparation of nursery-school through secondary-school teachers (programs resulting in the recommendation for professional certification), whether they are four-year, five-year or M.A.T. programs; and/or

2. *All advanced programs:* programs beyond the baccalaureate level for the advanced preparation of teachers and for the preparation of other professional school personnel.

NCATE Standards and Institutional Reports

Each of the standards which follows has a preamble which gives the rationale for the standard, interprets its meaning, and defines terms. The preamble therefore is to be interpreted as part of the standard which it precedes. Following each standard are questions designed to elicit information and evidence to show the extent to which the institution possesses the characteristics identified in the standard and its preamble.

Institutions of higher education seeking accreditation or re-accreditation by NCATE are expected to prepare a report based on the preambles, standards, and questions which follow the standards. It is expected that all of the questions will be answered in the institution's report. It is not assumed, however, that the questions included for each standard are exhaustive; an institution may provide other information to show that it possesses the characteristics described in a standard and its preamble.

Institutional Experimentation and Innovation

Responsible experimentation and innovation are essential to improvement of teacher education programs. A deliberate attempt has been made in these standards to encourage individuality, imagination, and innovation in institutional planning. An institution must, of course, assume responsibility for the quality of all its programs, regular and experimental.

Colleges and universities are responding to pressing social needs by developing programs to prepare teachers with special competencies or to prepare new types of teachers. These programs are subject to the same scrutiny as are the other teacher education programs offered by the institution. In some instances, the standards as organized may not provide the best vehicle for assessing such programs. In these cases, the institution is invited to present its experimental or special programs separately. Such presentations should include the rationale for the design of the programs, for admitting students who do not meet the usual criteria for admission, for using faculty members who do not meet the usual requirements for appointment to the full-time faculty, and should show that systematic efforts are being made to evaluate the graduates of these programs.

Part I: Basic Teacher Education Programs

Programs for the Initial Preparation of Teachers Through the Fifth-Year Level, Including M.A.T. Programs

1. Curricula for Basic Programs

Curricula for teacher education are designed to achieve explicitly stated objectives. These objectives are determined in relation to both the professional roles for which the preparation programs are designed and the behavioral outcomes sought. It is assumed that the design of each curriculum for the preparation of teachers adopted by the institution reflects the judgment of appropriate members of the faculty and staff, of students, of graduates, and of the profession as a whole. It is also assumed that these curricula reflect an awareness of research and development in teacher education.

Colleges and universities are responding to current pressing social needs by developing programs to prepare teachers with special competencies such as teachers for bilingual children, teachers for "disadvantaged children," teachers to work in teaching teams, teachers to teach in ungraded schools, and teachers with an international component as part of their training. These programs, often special or experimental in nature, are subject to the same scrutiny as are the other teacher education programs offered by the institution. In some instances, the standards, as organized, may not provide the best vehicle for reviewing such programs. In these cases, the institution is invited to present its experimental or special programs separately as noted in the Introduction.

As used in the following standards, a "teacher education program" refers to the curriculum, the teaching, the learning, and the supporting resources for the teaching and learning process. "Curriculum" includes the courses, seminars, readings, laboratory and clinical experiences, and practicum as described under the general studies component and the professional studies component. A "program of study" refers to the sequence of courses, seminars, readings, laboratory and clinical experiences, and practicum selected for each student.

1.1 Design of Curricula

Curricula for the preparation of teachers are composed of several components combined in patterns designed to achieve the objectives sought. These patterns are based on assumptions which can be identified by the institution and which reveal themselves in what is done in classroom, laboratory, and field experiences.

Standard: *Teacher education curricula are based on objectives reflecting the institution's conception of the teacher's role, and are organized to include general studies, content for the teaching specialty, humanistic and behavioral studies, teaching and learning theory with laboratory and clinical experience, and practicum.*

1.1.1 What information shows that each basic teacher education program is designed to achieve objectives reflecting the institution's analysis of the teacher's role?

1.1.2 What information shows that each curriculum in teacher education includes the elements identified in the standard?

1.2 The General Studies Component

Prospective teachers, like all other students, need a sound general education. However, their need is accentuated by the nature of the professional responsibilities that they are expected to assume. As teachers, they are destined to play an important role in providing general education for the children and youth they teach, and to serve as adequate models of educated persons to their students. Furthermore, the subjects studied in general education may be needed to support their teaching specialties.

Institutional programs of general or liberal studies vary widely although certain elements are usually present in all of them. Such variation precludes prescribing the general studies in terms of subject and credit hours. The view reflected in the standard is that general education should include the studies most widely generalizable. Far more important than the specific content of the general studies is that they be taught with emphasis upon generalization rather than with academic specialization as a primary objective. It is assumed, moreover, that programs of study in general education are individualized according to the needs and interests of students. It is further assumed that the selection of content for the general studies component is determined jointly by faculty members in the academic areas and those in teacher education.

As used in the standard, "symbolics of information" is that part of the general studies which deals with communication through symbols, including studies in such areas as languages, communication skills, linguistics, mathematics, logic, and information theory. "Natural and behavioral sciences" and "humanities" follow their common usage in higher education.

It is the intent of the standard to designate a minimum limit for general studies and to encourage institutions to exceed it. "One-third," as specified in the standards, is applicable to four-year curricula for prospective teachers.

Standard: *There is a planned general studies component requiring that at least one-third of each curriculum for prospective teachers consist of studies in the symbolics of information, natural and behavioral sciences, and humanities.*

> 1.2.1 What courses, seminars, and readings are offered in each area of general studies identified in the standard?
>
> 1.2.2 What are the arrangements for ensuring that courses, seminars, and readings are distributed among the areas of general studies as specified in the standard?
>
> 1.2.3 What evidence shows that the program of study of each student meets the institution's requirements in general studies?
>
> 1.2.4 What evidence (such as state and regional accreditation reports and/or student achievement data) reflects the quality of the general studies component?
>
> 1.2.5 What information shows that some initial assessment is made of the level and quality of the general education background of each student and that each program of study is accordingly individualized?
>
> 1.2.6 How does the institution ensure that the selection of content for the general studies component embodies the judgment of both the academic staff and the teacher education faculty?

1.3 The Professional Studies Component

The professional part of a curriculum designed to prepare teachers should be distinguishable from the general studies component: the latter includes whatever instruction is deemed desirable for all students, regardless of their prospective occupation; the former—professional—component covers all requirements that are justified by the work of the specific profession of teaching. In the standards that follow it is assumed, therefore, that the classification of a study as general or professional does not depend on the name of the study or the department in which the instruction is offered; it depends rather on the function the study is to perform.

The designation of the elements in the professional studies component (as delineated in standards 1.3.1 through 1.3.4) is not intended to prescribe a particular design for teacher education. Rather, it is intended to provide a set of categories through which an institution can describe and review the professional studies component of the various teacher education curricula it offers. It is assumed that these elements can be identified in any acceptable design for teacher education.

1.3.1 Content for the Teaching Specialty. The "Content for the Teaching Specialty" is included in the professional studies component of the curriculum to direct attention to the central importance of appropriate subject matter in a teaching specialty in the professional preparation of the teacher. It does not imply that such subject matter should be professionalized nor that the instruction should be provided in any specific school or department or in any particular format, such as "courses." The instruction in the subject matter for the teaching specialties is the basic responsibility of the respective academic departments; the identification and selection of courses and other learning experiences required for a teaching specialty, however, are the joint responsibility of appropriate members of the faculty in the teaching specialty concerned and members of the teacher education faculty. Joint responsibility for determining the content of a teaching specialty should result in content that is peculiarly relevant to teaching.

The standard draws attention to the fact that teaching requires two types of knowledge which may extend beyond what is required in general studies. One is the knowledge that is to be taught to the pupil; the other is the knowledge that may be needed by the teacher as a background for the teaching of his particular specialty. It is assumed in the standard that both kinds of knowledge are a required part of the candidate's professional training.

"Teaching specialty" as used in the standard includes elementary education as a specialized field as well as the various specializations offered in the secondary school.

Standard: *The professional studies component of each curriculum for prospective teachers includes the study of the content to be taught to pupils; and the supplementary knowledge, from the subject matter of the teaching specialty and from allied fields, that is needed by the teacher for perspective and flexibility in teaching.*

> 1.3.1 a What evidence shows that the program of study of each prospective teacher includes both types of content for the teaching specialty identified in the standard?
>
> 1.3.1 b What information shows that the selection of courses and other learning experiences required for the teaching specialty in each

curriculum embodies the judgment of members of the faculty in the teaching specialty concerned and members of the teacher education faculty?

1.3.1 c What are the provisions for ensuring that a systematic effort is made to keep the content of the respective teaching specialties current with developments in the appropriate disciplines as they relate to teaching?

1.3.2 Humanistic and Behavioral Studies. Many disciplines are important in the preparation of teachers. However, not all disciplines are equally relevant, and their relevance is not always obvious. In the following standard it is assumed that problems concerning the nature and aims of education, the curriculum, the organization and administration of a school system, and the process of teaching and learning can be studied with respect to their historical development and the philosophical issues to which they are related. These studies are referred to hereafter as the humanistic studies. The problems of education can also be studied with respect to the findings and methods of psychology, sociology, anthropology, economics, and political science. Such studies are referred to as behavioral studies. These humanistic and behavioral studies differ from the usual study of history, philosophy, psychology, sociology, anthropology, economics, and political science in that they address themselves to the problems of education. The major purpose of such studies is to provide the student with a set of contexts in which educational problems can be understood and interpreted.

The humanistic and behavioral studies require a familiarity with the parent disciplines on which they are based. This familiarity may be acquired as part of the general studies and/or as part of the content for the teaching specialty.

The standard does not imply that instruction in the humanistic and behavioral studies should be organized or structured in a particular way. Instruction in these studies may be offered in such courses as history and/or philosophy of education, educational sociology, psychology of education; or as an integral part of such courses as history, philosophy, psychology, sociology; or as topics in foundation courses, problems in education courses, or in professional block programs; or as independent readings.

Standard: *The professional studies component of each curriculum for prospective teachers includes instruction in the humanistic studies and the behavioral studies.*

1.3.2 a What humanistic and behavioral studies are part of the professional component of each curriculum, and what is the supporting rationale for including them?

1.3.2 b What information shows that these studies are oriented toward the problems of education, such as the nature and aims of education, curriculum, organization and administration, teaching and learning?

1.3.2 c What information shows that the instruction in the humanistic and behavioral studies incorporates the findings of research and scholarly writings, and provides experiences for students in their interpretation and use?

1.3.2 d What data show that the programs of study of all prospective teachers include the humanistic and behavioral studies prescribed by the institution?

1.3.3 Teaching and Learning Theory with Laboratory and Clinical Experience. As distinguished from the Content for the Teaching Specialty and the Humanistic and Behavioral Studies, there is a body of knowledge about teaching and learning that should be the basis for effective performance. If teaching is to be more than a craft, teachers need to understand the theoretical principles which explain what they do. For this reason, the study of teaching and learning theory is included as part of the professional studies component. However, like the study of other empirical theory, the study of teaching and learning theory requires laboratory experiences through which the student may conceptualize principles and interpret their application to practical problems. Much of what has been called "general methods" and "special methods" can therefore be taught as the application of teaching and learning theory.

Whereas the study of teaching and learning theory provides the prospective teacher with principles of practice, and the laboratory exercises illuminate and demonstrate these principles, clinical experience confronts the student with individual cases or problems, the diagnosis and solution of which involve the application of principles and theory. Certain kinds of problems (such as planning, selection of learning resources, motivation, presentation, diagnosis of learning difficulties, individualization of instruction, classroom management, and evaluation) represent recurring types of classroom situations. Clinical teaching involves the student in the diagnosis and "treatment" of the individual problem, under the guidance of an experienced teacher. Because it is now possible to simulate many of these situations or to display a selection of real problems electronically—and because the prospective teacher's efforts can be recorded, viewed, and reviewed —it is now feasible to give much effective clinical experience outside the school classroom.

Standard: *The professional studies component of each curriculum includes the systematic study of teaching and learning theory with appropriate laboratory and clinical experience.*

1.3.3 a In what courses, seminars, and readings are provisions made for the study of teaching and learning theory?

1.3.3 b What practices or procedures show that the study of teaching and learning theory requires and is accompanied by laboratory experiences (observation, demonstration, problem-solving, tutoring, microteaching, and/or other direct experiential activities)?

1.3.3 c What are the provisions for clinical experience (diagnosing and treating individual typical cases, practices, or problems)?

1.3.3 d What information shows that the instruction in the study of teaching and learning theory incorporates the findings of research and other scholarly writings, and provides experiences for students in their interpretation and use?

1.3.3 e What data indicate that all prospective teachers have laboratory and clinical experiences under the guidance of an experienced teacher?

1.3.3 f What evidence shows that the programs of study of all prospective teachers include the systematic study of teaching and learning theory with appropriate laboratory and clinical experience?

1.3.4 Practicum. "Practicum" refers to a period of experience in professional practice during which the student tests and reconstructs the theory which he has evolved and during which he further develops his own teaching style. It provides an opportunity for the student to assume major responsibility for the full range of teaching duties in a real school situation under the guidance of qualified personnel from the institution and from the cooperating elementary or secondary school. It presupposes the learning experiences included in all other professional studies; it is not a substitute for them. It is a more complete and concrete learning activity than laboratory and clinical experience.

It is assumed that the institution carefully selects the cooperating schools used for practicum and that it establishes effective working arrangements with these schools.

Practicum in most situations may be called student teaching; in some situations it may be a type of internship.

Standard: *The professional studies component of each curriculum for prospective teachers includes direct substantial participation in teaching over an extended period of time under the supervision of qualified personnel from the institution and the cooperating school.*

1.3.4 a What evidence shows that every prospective teacher assumes substantial responsibility over an extended period of time for the range of teaching duties in the professional role for which he is being prepared?

1.3.4 b What information shows that relationships between professional personnel in the institution and in the cooperating schools contribute positively to students' experience in practicum?

1.3.4 c What evidence confirms that the supervision of students in practicum is organized and executed under the direction of qualified personnel from the institution?

1.3.4 d What information shows that the supervising teachers in the cooperating schools are superior teachers, are trained in supervision, and are committed to the task of educating teachers?

1.3.4 e What systematic methods are used to record or describe the teaching performance of students and how is the resulting data used by students and supervisors to analyze teaching behavior?

1.3.4 f How is the supervision of students in practicum translated into an index of faculty load? For how many students in practicum does each teacher education faculty member have responsibility?

1.4 Use of Guidelines Developed by National Learned Societies and Professional Associations

National learned societies and professional associations with special interest in curricula for the preparation of teachers have significant contributions to make to the improvement of teacher education programs. On the basis of extensive study and research, some of these organizations have developed guidelines for the preparation of teachers. It is expected that an institution will work out the rationale for its various teacher education curricula with due consideration given to such guidelines appropriate to the elements in the professional studies component. Due consideration means that the institution is acquainted with these guidelines and has critically examined them in relation to developing the teacher education curricula offered.

Standard: *In planning and developing curricula for teacher education, the institution gives due consideration to guidelines for teacher preparation developed by national learned societies and professional associations.*

1.4.1 What guidelines has the institution considered in developing the following elements of the professional studies component:
   a. The content for each teaching specialty offered?
   b. The humanistic and behavioral studies?
   c. Teaching and learning theory with laboratory and clinical experience?
   d. Practicum?

1.4.2 What information shows that the guidelines identified in 1.4.1 have been critically examined in relation to the planning and development of the curricula offered?

1.5 Control of Basic Programs

Administrative structure exists primarily as a practical arrangement for formulating and achieving goals, fixing responsibility, utilizing resources, and facilitating continuous development and improvement. The standard assumes that this principle is applicable to administrative units responsible for the preparation of teachers. It is expected that the particular unit within the institution officially designated as responsible for teacher education is composed of persons who have experience in, and commitment to, the task of educating teachers.

The standard does not prescribe any particular organizational structure. A unit as referred to below may take the form of a council, commission, committee, department, school, college, or other recognizable organizational entity.

While major responsibility for designing, approving, evaluating, and developing teacher education programs is carried by an officially designated unit, it is assumed that teacher education faculty members are systematically involved in the decision-making process.

Standard: *The design, approval, and continuous evaluation and development of teacher education programs are the primary responsibility of an officially designated unit; the majority of the membership of this unit is composed of faculty and/or staff members who are significantly involved in teacher education.*

1.5.1 What administrative unit within the institution has primary responsibility for the preparation of teachers and what is the rationale for determining its membership and responsibilities?

1.5.2 What evidence shows that the majority of the membership of the official unit is made up of faculty and/or staff members significantly involved in teacher education?

1.5.3 What activities of the official unit during the past two years demonstrate that it has assumed responsibility for the design, approval, and continuous evaluation and development of each teacher education program offered by the institution?

1.5.4 What information shows that teacher education faculty members share in the decision-making process in matters related to designing, evaluating, and developing teacher education programs?

2. Faculty for Basic Programs

Teacher education programs require a competent faculty which has been systematically developed into a coherent body devoted to the preparation of effective teachers. The faculty is significantly involved in the evaluation and development of teacher education programs offered by the institution and is engaged in systematic efforts to improve the quality of instruction provided. The faculty constantly scrutinizes curricula in relation to the characteristics and needs of the students enrolled and in relation to the resources required to support the offering of acceptable programs. The following standards deal with significant aspects of faculty competence in relation to the development, execution, and review of teacher education programs; and with conditions for effective faculty performance.

"Faculty for teacher education" as used in standards 2.1 through 2.4 includes those faculty members responsible for the instruction in humanistic and behavioral studies, in teaching and learning theory with laboratory and clinical experience, and in practicum.

2.1 Competence and Utilization of Faculty

The competence of the faculty is the crucial factor in teacher education, not only for the quality of instruction which is provided, but also for the total atmosphere in which the programs are implemented. Above all, the quality of teacher education programs offered, and the degree to which such quality is maintained, depend primarily on the faculty.

The competence of faculty is established on the basis of academic preparation, experience, teaching, and scholarly performance. The standard assumes that advanced graduate work in a well-defined field of specialization, taken in a regionally accredited institution or a recognized foreign institution, is the minimal requirement for teaching in a collegiate institution. In certain cases, where the faculty member has not completed the requisite advanced graduate work, competence may be established on the basis of scholarly performance as reflected by publication, research, and/or recognition by professional peers in the faculty member's field of specialization.

An institution capitalizes on the academic and professional strength of its faculty by making assignments which make possible the maximum use of preparation and experience. An institution also relates faculty selection and assignment to faculty performance.

The standard does not preclude the offering of adequate programs of teacher education with a small faculty, but it does discourage the over-extension of faculty and the use of faculty in areas in which they are not competent. The standard does not require that faculty members be assigned to a particular school or department within the institution.

Standard: *An institution engaged in preparing teachers has full-time faculty members in teacher education, each with post-master's degree preparation and/or demonstrated scholarly competence, and each with appropriate specializations. Such specializations make possible competent instruction in the humanistic and behavioral studies, in teaching and learning theory, and in the methods of teaching in each of the specialties for which the institution prepares teachers. There are appropriate specializations to ensure competent supervision of laboratory, clinical, and practicum experiences.*

2.1.1 What evidence indicates that there is a full-time faculty for teacher education with qualifications requisite to competent instruction in each of the areas specified in the standard?

2.1.2 What evidence shows that all courses and other learning experiences in each of the areas specified in the standard are actually conducted by faculty members appropriately prepared to do so?

2.1.3 If any faculty members have been teaching in fields for which they are not qualified, for how long and for what special reasons has this been permitted?

2.1.4 What is done to evaluate the effectivness of the instruction in each of the areas specified in the standard?

2.2 Faculty Involvement with Schools

Faculty members who instruct prospective teachers need frequent contacts with school environments so that their teaching and research are current and relevant. In addition, the commitment of a teacher education faculty is to the needs of the teaching profession as a whole as well as to institutional programs. It is assumed that elementary and secondary school personnel share with faculty members in colleges and universities a common purpose and interest in teacher education. The specialized talent of the teacher education faculty is viewed as a potential resource for providing in-service assistance to the schools in the area served by the institution.

Standard: *Members of the teacher education faculty have continuing association and involvement with elementary and secondary schools.*

2.2.1 In what ways have members of the faculty for teacher education been associated and involved with activities of elementary and secondary schools?

2.2.2 What information shows that such association and involvement are reflected in the institution's teacher education programs?

2.2.3 What information indicates that the special competencies of the teacher education faculty are reflected in the services offered to the schools?

2.3 Conditions for Faculty Service

The institution, recognizing that the faculty is the major determinant of the quality of its teacher education programs, makes provision for the efficient use of faculty competence, time, and energy. Such provisions include policies which establish maximum limits for teaching loads, permit adjustments in teaching loads when nonteaching duties are assigned, and allow time for the faculty member to do the planning involved in carrying out his assigned responsibilities.

To maintain and to improve the quality of its faculty, the institution has a plan for faculty development which provides such opportunities as in-service education, sabbatical leave, travel support, summer leaves, intra- and inter-institutional visitation, and fellowships. In addition, time is allocated in the load of a faculty member so that he can continue his scholarly development.

The institution recognizes that the quality of its instructional programs can be compromised if faculty members are dissipating their energy on subprofessional tasks. Therefore, provision is made for supporting services (such as those provided by instructional media technicians, laboratory and/or instructional assistants, research assistants, and secretaries and clerks) that permit faculty members to fulfill their instructional and other professional responsibilities at a high level of performance.

Standard: *The institution provides conditions essential to the effective performance by the teacher education faculty.*

2.3.1 What is the plan and its supporting rationale for taking into account all professional duties and activities of the faculty in determining load?

2.3.2 What is the assigned professional load (all services rendered) for each teacher education faculty member?

2.3.3 If the load of any faculty member exceeds the established institutional policy, for how long and for what reasons has this been permitted

2.3.4 What program does the institution have for faculty development and what evidence shows that it is operative?

2.3.5 What is the plan for allocating supporting services to the faculty and what evidence shows that such services are provided?

2.4 Part-Time Faculty

Two kinds of situations support the employment of faculty on a part-time basis. One is the need of the institution for a special competence not represented on the regular staff and not requiring a full-time faculty member. The other is the need for additional service in areas of competence already represented on the full-time staff. However, in the interests of operating acceptable programs, the institution prevents the fragmentation of instruction and the erosion of program quality that can accompany excessive use of part-time faculty. It is assumed that the competence of part-time faculty as indicated by academic preparation, experience, teaching, and scholarly performance is comparable to that of full-time faculty.

Standard: *Part-time faculty meet the requirements for appointment to the full-time faculty and are employed only when they can make special contributions to the teacher education programs.*

2.4.1 What are the qualifications of the part-time faculty members in teacher education, and what proportion of the instruction in each curriculum is assigned to them?

2.4.2 What is the load, within and without the institution, for each part-time faculty member in teacher education?

2.4.3 What reasons support the use of each part-time faculty member in teacher education?

2.4.4 What provisions are made to ensure that part-time faculty members are oriented to the basic purposes of, and kept abreast of, current developments in the institution's teacher education programs?

3. Students in Basic Programs

Teacher education programs described above require students who have intellectual, emotional, and personal qualifications that promise to result in successful performance in the profession. Attention to the characteristics of students admitted to, retained in, and graduated from teacher education is essential to designing and maintaining acceptable programs. It is assumed that an institution selects and retains qualified students in its programs and eliminates those who should not go into teaching; that it provides counseling and advising services; that it provides opportunities for student participation in the evaluation and development of programs; and that it evaluates graduates. The evaluation of graduates is treated in another section of the standards.

In certain instances, institutions may wish to recognize the potential existing in students who do not qualify for admission by the usual criteria by offering special or experimental teacher education programs. In such cases, institutions will explain fully the rationale underlying admission and retention of students in these programs.

3.1 Admission to Basic Programs

Students seeking admission to programs of teacher education may have to meet requirements in addition to those generally prescribed for enrollment in the institution because there are skills, understandings, and personal characteristics which are unique to teaching. The institution, therefore, uses a number of criteria for admitting students to its teacher education programs. These criteria, both objective and subjective, reflect a rational process for selecting students whose success in the profession can be reasonably predicted.

No single criterion can as yet predict success or failure. This applies to scores on objective tests as well as to more subjective criteria. Nevertheless, scores on standardized tests are useful in predicting the probability of success in the program of studies prescribed for teacher education. Test scores also provide a basis on which institutions can determine how students entering their programs compare with external indicators of probable success.

The following standard applies to the selection of students in regular teacher education programs. For experimental or special programs, specific admission requirements should be indicated in the description of these programs.

Standard: *The institution applies specific criteria for admission to teacher education programs; these criteria require the use of both objective and subjective data.*

3.1.1 What are the requirements for admission to the teacher education programs and what is the supporting rationale?

3.1.2 What evidence shows that the admission requirements are being met?

3.1.3 How many students applied for admission to teacher education during the past two years? How many were denied admission? How many who were denied admission were subsequently admitted, and for what reasons?

3.1.4 What objective data, including tests results with national norms, are used for admitting students to teacher education programs?

3.1.5 If the institution admits students who do not meet its usual admission criteria, what special resources does it devote to the remediation or enrichment necessary to enable some of these students to meet the institutional requirements for admission to teacher education programs?

3.1.6 What characteristics of the students admitted are revealed by the data obtained through applying objective and subjective admission criteria?

3.2 Retention of Students in Basic Programs

The nature of the professional studies component in teacher education curricula calls for a high order of academic achievement and growth in technical competence. Grades in course work provide the usual measures of achievement in theoretical work; observations, reports, and other modes of appraisal provide evaluations of laboratory, clinical and practicum experiences. The institution owes it to the student to determine as objectively and systematically as possible specific strengths and weaknesses as they affect his continuing in a teacher education program.

The academic competence of the teacher is a major determinant of effective teaching, but it is not the only one. Prospective teachers demonstrate those personal characteristics which will contribute to, rather than detract from, their performance in the classroom. It is assumed in the standard that the institution has the right and the obligation to consider personal factors as well as academic achievement as a basis for permitting a student to continue in a teacher education program.

Standard: *The institution applies specific criteria for the retention of candidates in basic programs who possess academic competencies and personal characteristics appropriate to the requirements of teaching.*

3.2.1 What objective means are used to evaluate the achievement of students in each area of the professional studies component of the teacher education programs?

3.2.2 What information other than course grades is used to evaluate the achievement of prospective teachers?

3.2.3 What requirements for academic competence must students meet to continue in the teacher education programs?

3.2.4 On the basis of what personal characteristics does the institution screen out students from the teacher education programs?

3.2.5 Under what circumstances, if any, are students who do not meet the institution's requirements for retention permitted to continue in the basic programs?

3.3 Counseling and Advising for Students in Basic Programs

Students planning to be teachers need counseling and advising services that supplement those regularly provided by the institution. Qualified counselors and advisors assist students in assessing their strengths and weaknesses and in planning their programs of study. Prospective teachers need to be informed about professional organizations and agencies as well as current school problems. They also need to know about the wide variety of options available to them in teaching. Graduates may need the help of the institution in finding appropriate teaching positions.

Standard: *The institution has a well-defined plan for counseling and advising students in teacher education.*

3.3.1 What special counseling and advising services are provided for students in teacher education?

3.3.2 What information shows that counselors and advisors for teacher education students know the nature and scope of the teaching profession, the problems of the schools, and the institutional resources available to students?

3.3.3 What information shows that the institution maintains a comprehensive system of records for all prospective teachers which is readily and easily available to faculty members and placement officers for professional purposes?

3.4 Student Participation in Program Evaluation and Development

As members of the college community, prospective teachers have the opportunity and responsibility to express their views regarding the improvement of teacher education programs. Through student organizations, through joint student-faculty groups, and/or through membership on faculty committees, they have clear channels and frequent opportunities to express their views with the assurance that their proposals will influence the development of the teacher education programs offered by the institution.

Standard: *The institution has representative student participation in the evaluation and development of its teacher education programs.*

3.4.1 What evidence shows that students participate in the evaluation and development of preparation programs offered by the institution?

3.4.2 What are the major concerns which students have expressed during the last two years and in what ways have these concerns influenced the development of teacher education programs?

4. Resources and Facilities for Basic Programs

The institution provides an environment which supports the basic teacher education programs it offers. The adequacy of this environment is systematically evaluated in relation to the demands made upon it by curricula, faculty, and students. In the standards, certain elements of this environment are selected for fuller explication without presuming to relegate other elements to insignificance and without assuming that those which are selected are of equal importance. The standards treat the importance of the library, the materials and instructional media center, and physical facilities and other resources in relation to the offering of acceptable teacher education programs.

4.1 Library

The library is viewed as the principal educational materials resource and information storage and retrieval center of an institution. As a principal resource for teaching and learning, the library holdings in teacher education are sufficient in number for the students served and pertinent to the types and levels of programs offered. The recommendations of faculty members and national professional organizations are seriously considered in maintaining and building the collection. Library service assures both students and faculty members access to the holdings.

Standard: *The library is adequate to support the instruction, research, and services pertinent to each teacher education program.*

4.1.1 What evidence shows that the library collection includes:
  a. Standard and contemporary holdings in education (books, microfilms, microfiche copies, etc.)?
  b. Standard periodicals in education?
  c. Such additional specialized books, periodicals, and other resources needed to support each teacher education program?

4.1.2 What evidence shows that the institution, in maintaining and improving the quality of its library holdings in teacher education, seriously considers the recommendations of:
  a. Faculty?
  b. Appropriate national professional organizations and learned societies?
  c. A nationally recognized list (or lists) of books and periodicals?

4.1.3 What information indicates that both students and faculty have access to, and use, the library holdings?

4.1.4 What is the annual record of library expenditures for the total library and for teacher education during the past five years?

4.2 Materials and Instructional Media Center

Modern media and materials are essential elements in the communications system of contemporary society. For this reason, teachers need to understand the technologies that make such media and materials usable in their teaching and need to possess skills in using them. As a means to assist prospective teachers in developing these understandings and skills, the institution makes available to students and faculty members appropriate teaching-learning materials and instructional media. In maintaining and developing the collection of such materials and media, the institution gives serious consideration to the recommendations of faculty members and appropriate national professional organizations.

A program for the preparation of teachers includes the use of teaching-learning materials and instructional media in two important ways: prospective teachers are instructed how to devise and use modern technologies in their teaching, and modern technologies are utilized by the faculty in teaching students.

Standard: *A materials and instructional media center for teacher education is maintained either as a part of the library, or as one or more separate units, and is adequate to support the teacher education programs.*

4.2.1 What information shows that the center contains materials and equipment that:
  a. Are utilized at different grade levels in elementary and secondary schools?
  b. Are utilized for teaching and learning in the teacher education curricula offered by the institution?
  c. Are representative of the teaching specialties offered by the institution?
  d. Reflect recent developments in the teaching of the various subject fields?
  e. Illustrate the wide array of available instructional media (such as films, filmstrips, realia, audiovideo tapes, transparencies, teaching machines, and closed-circuit TV)?

4.2.2 What evidence shows that the institution, in maintaining and improving the quality of the center, seriously considers the recommendations of:
  a. Faculty and staff members?
  b. Appropriate national professional organizations?

4.2.3 What information shows that the center is directed by personnel who are knowledgeable about instructional media and materials?

4.2.4 What information indicates that the center is available to and used by:
  a. Students?
  b. Teacher education faculty members?

4.3 Physical Facilities and Other Resources

Basic teacher education programs draw on the full range of institutional resources to support instruction and research. Assuming that the other aspects of an institution's teacher education programs are acceptable, the adequacy of the physical facilities, equipment, and special resources is judged in terms of the operational requirements of the basic programs offered. It is assumed that such facilities and resources are readily accessible so that faculty and students may effectively pursue instructional objectives.

Standard: *The institution provides physical facilities and other resources essential to the instructional and research activities of each basic program.*

4.3.1 What facts indicate that for each basic teacher education program offered, faculty and students have office space, instructional space, and other space necessary to carry out their responsibilities?

4.3.2 What information shows that the institution draws on the full range of its resources to support its basic programs?

4.3.3 What information indicates that the institution has given serious consideration to the recommendations of faculty members for improving physical facilities and other supporting resources?

5. Evaluation, Program Review, and Planning

Maintenance of acceptable teacher education programs demands a continuous process of evaluation of the graduates of existing programs, modification of existing programs, and long-range planning. It is assumed that faculty and administrators in teacher education evaluate the result of their programs and relate the findings of this evaluation to program development. This requires the continuous review of the institution's objectives for its teacher education programs. It is also assumed that, in its plans for total institutional development, the institution projects plans for the long-range development of teacher education.

5.1 Evaluation of Graduates

Criteria for admission and retention provide some assurance that students of promise and ability enter and continue in teacher education programs. Such criteria do not ensure that students of promise and ability will complete the programs, nor that they will enter the teaching profession, nor that they will perform satisfactorily after becoming teachers. The ultimate criterion for judging a teacher education program is whether it produces competent graduates who enter the profession and perform effectively. An institution committed to the preparation of teachers engages in systematic efforts to evaluate the quality of its graduates and those persons recommended for professional certification. The institution evaluates the teachers it produces at two critical points: when they complete their programs of study, and after they enter the teaching profession.

It is recognized that the means now available for making such evaluations are not fully adequate. Nevertheless, the standard assumes that an institution evaluates the teachers it prepares with the best means now available, and that it attempts to develop improved means for making such evaluations. As progress is made toward more adequate evaluation procedures, this standard will become increasingly important.

Any effort to assess the quality of graduates requires that evaluations be made in relation to the objectives sought. Therefore, institutions use the stated objectives of their teacher education programs as a basis for evaluating the teachers they prepare.

Standard: *The institution conducts a well-defined plan for evaluating the teachers it prepares.*

5.1.1 What information shows that the stated objectives for the teacher education programs are used as a basis for evaluating the teachers prepared by the institution?

5.1.2 What means are used to collect data about teachers prepared in the various programs (graduates and persons recommended for certification):
   a. At the point when programs of study are completed?
   b. After they enter the teaching profession?

5.1.3 What information shows that the institution is keeping abreast of new developments in the evaluation of teacher education graduates and is engaged in efforts to improve its plan for making such evaluations?

5.1.4 What percent of the teachers prepared by the institution during the last two years actually entered the teaching profession?

5.1.5 What characteristics of teachers prepared by the institution have been revealed through evaluation of graduates?

5.2 Use of Evaluation Results to Improve Basic Programs

The institution evaluates the teachers it prepares not only to obtain assessments of their quality, but also to provide information to identify areas in the programs that need strengthening and to suggest new directions for program development. It is assumed in the standard that the results of the evaluations made by the institution are reflected in modifications in the preparation programs.

Standard: *The institution uses the evaluation results in the study, development, and improvement of its teacher education programs.*

    5.2.1 What strengths and weaknesses in the teacher education programs are revealed as a result of evaluating teachers prepared by the institution?

    5.2.2 What does the institution do to ensure that the results obtained from evaluating the teachers it prepares are translated into appropriate program modifications?

5.3 Long-Range Planning

Institutional plans for future development provide a basis for making decisions in such matters as increasing or limiting enrollment, introducing new programs, expanding and strengthening existing programs, or entering the field of graduate education. Effective long-range planning presupposes that the institution periodically engages in study and research to ascertain whether its present policies and practices are an effective means for accomplishing its purposes. It is assumed that the institutional community will participate in conducting such studies and in projecting plans for the long-range development of teacher education.

Standard: *The institution has plans for the long-range development of teacher education; these plans are part of a design for total institutional development.*

    5.3.1 What evidence indicates that the institution has, or is engaged in, studies and/or research to improve its teacher education programs?

    5.3.2 What information shows that the faculty for teacher education participates in the formulation of the institution's long-range plans for teacher education?

    5.3.3 What is the institution's plan for future development of basic teacher education programs and what rationale supports significant changes that are proposed?

Part II: Advanced Programs

Post-Baccalaureate Programs for the Advanced Preparation of Teachers and the Preparation of Other Professional School Personnel

G-1. Curricula for Advanced Programs

Curricula for advanced programs are designed to achieve explicitly stated objectives. These objectives are expressed behaviorally and are determined in relation to the professional roles for which the preparation programs are designed. The satisfactory completion of the studies prescribed for a curriculum culminates in an appropriate certificate or degree.

Colleges and universities are responding to current pressing social needs by developing new kinds of programs for the preparation of professional school personnel at the graduate level. These programs, often special or experimental in nature, are subject to the same scrutiny as are the other advanced programs offered by the institution. In some instances the standards, as organized, may not provide the best vehicle for assessing such programs. In these cases, the institution is invited to present its experimental or special programs separately as noted in the Introduction.

As used in these standards, "other professional school personnel" refers to such personnel as superintendents, principals, curriculum specialists, supervisors, and counselors. An "advanced program" refers to a graduate program for the advanced preparation of teachers and/or the preparation of other professional school personnel, and includes the curriculum, the teaching, the learning, and the supporting resources for the teaching and learning process. "Curriculum" includes the courses, seminars, readings, direct and simulated experiences in professional practice (laboratory, clinical, practicum, assistantship, internship, etc.), and research, as categorized in standards G-1.1, G-1.2, and G-1.3. A "program of study" refers to the sequence of courses, seminars, readings, and the direct and simulated experiences in professional practice selected for each graduate student enrolled in an advanced program.

G-1.1 Design of Curricula

Curricula for the advanced preparation of teachers and for the preparation of other professional school personnel are composed of several components combined in patterns designed to achieve the objectives sought. These patterns are based upon assumptions which can be identified by the institution and which reveal themselves in what is done in classroom, laboratory, and field experiences. These patterns are designed so that the instruction offered is appropriate to the degree level (master's, sixth-year, or doctoral) of the various advanced programs. In addition, the design of the patterns provides for the individualization of programs of study. The components of advanced curricula may be described in a variety of ways. In the standards which follow, they are identified as content for the specialty, humanistic and behavioral studies, theory relevant to the specialty with direct and simulated experiences in professional practice, and research.

Standard: *Curricula for advanced programs are based on objectives reflecting the institution's conception of the professional roles for which the preparation programs are designed.*

G-1.1.1 For what professional school position does each advanced program prepare personnel (school superintendent, principal, supervisor, specialist, teacher, and/or other positions)?

G-1.1.2 What evidence indicates that specific objectives for the curriculum of each advanced program have been defined and that these objectives reflect the institution's analysis of the professional school position for which candidates are being prepared?

G-1.2 Content of Curricula

Curricula for advanced programs are designed to prepare personnel for different types of school positions and at different degree levels. For this reason, components that are common to such curricula are identified only in terms of general categories of learning experiences as follows: content for the specialty, humanistic and behavioral studies, theory relevant to the specialty with direct and simulated experiences in professional practice, and research. The identification of these categories does not preclude the patterning of programs of study to meet the needs of individual students. The individualization of programs of study is treated in another standard.

The "content for the specialty" component for teachers includes advanced study in the subject matter to be taught and in allied fields. For other professional school personnel, this component includes studies in the specialization area and in allied fields.

The "humanistic and behavioral studies" in all advanced curricula include studies that have as their major purpose providing the student with a set of contexts in which educational problems can be understood and interpreted at a level beyond that required for the initial preparation of teachers. As in basic programs, the problems of education can be studied with respect to their historical development and the philosophical issues to which they are related, and they can also be studied with respect to the findings and methods of behavioral and social sciences. These humanistic and behavioral studies are unique in that they address themselves to the problems of education. The standard does not imply that instruction in the humanistic and behavioral studies should be organized or structured in a particular way. Instruction in these studies may be offered in such courses and seminars as history and/or philosophy of education, educational sociology, psychology of education; or as an integral part of such courses and seminars as history, philosophy, psychology, sociology; or as topics in foundation courses and seminars; or as independent readings or research. In some cases these studies may be part of the content of the specialty.

The "theory with practice" component for teachers includes advanced studies that draw on the body of knowledge about teaching and learning theory. For other professional school personnel, this component includes studies in theory relevant to the particular professional role for which candidates are preparing. Such studies are included so that school personnel can understand the theoretical principles which explain what they do in their professional roles. However, like the study of other empirical theory, the study of "theory relevant to the specialty" requires related experiences in professional practice through which the student may conceptualize principles and interpret their application to practical problems, and through which he further develops his individual style in professional practice.

"Research" as a component in advanced curricula is given special attention in standard G-1.3.

Standard: *The curriculum of each advanced program includes (a) content for the specialty, (b) humanistic and behavioral studies, (c) theory relevant to the specialty with direct and simulated experiences in professional practice, all appropriate to the professional roles for which candidates are being prepared and all differentiated by degree or certificate level.*

G-1.2.1 What information shows that the curriculum of each advanced program includes:
   a. Appropriate content for the specialty?
   b. Humanistic and behavioral studies?
   c. Theory relevant to the specialty?

G-1.2.2 What information shows that the curriculum of each advanced program includes direct and simulated experiences in professional practice which relate significantly to the school position for which the preparation program is designed?

G-1.2.3 How are the studies and experiences in professional practice that are prescribed for the curriculum of each advanced program differentiated by degree or certificate level?

G-1.2.4 What evidence indicates that candidates for degrees or certificates in each advanced program during the last two years have completed the studies and practice experiences identified in the standard?

G-1.3 Research in Advanced Curricula

Research in any discipline or field constitutes an organized effort to solve problems, to advance knowledge, and to test theories. Teachers and other professional school personnel need to have continuous access to research findings, to know how to understand and evaluate them, and to demonstrate skill in adapting them to professional needs. Training in research methods, interpretation, evaluation, and application varies with the degree offered and with the demands of the professional role for which the candidate is preparing.

Standard: *Each advanced curriculum includes the study of research methods and findings; each doctoral curriculum includes the designing and conducting of research.*

G-1.3.1 What provisions are made for including the research component in the curriculum of each advanced program?

G-1.3.2 What information shows that the requirements for research are relevant to the professional role for which the student is preparing?

G-1.3.3 What data show that the requirements for research are met in each student's program of study?

G-1.4 Individualization of Programs of Study

Curricula for advanced programs are individualized—that is, they are translated into programs of study which meet the particular needs of each student. This means that, while the programs of study for all students in a particular advanced program have common elements, the mix of these elements will vary for individual programs of study. To capitalize upon the strengths students bring to the program, to provide opportunities for expression of personal and professional interests, and to make available means whereby each student may improve in areas of weakness, demand great flexibility in planning programs of study.

Standard: *Each advanced curriculum provides for the individualization of students' programs of study.*

G-1.4.1 What data are used to ascertain the professional needs and interests of each candidate at the time of admission and subsequently, as necessary?

G-1.4.2 What evidence shows that programs of study have been planned to meet individual professional needs and interests?

G-1.5 Use of Guidelines Developed by National Learned Societies and Professional Associations

National learned societies and professional associations with special interest in curricula for the preparation of school personnel have significant contributions to make to the improvement of advanced programs. On the basis of extensive study and research, some of these organizations have developed guidelines for the advanced preparation of teachers and other professional school personnel. It is expected that an institution will work out the rationale for its advanced curricula with due consideration given to such guidelines appropriate to the respective advanced programs offered. Due consideration means that the institution is acquainted with these guidelines and has examined them critically in relation to developing its advanced curricula.

Standard: *In planning and developing curricula for its advanced programs, the institution gives due consideration to guidelines developed by national learned societies and professional associations for the preparation of teachers and other professional school personnel.*

G-1.5.1 What guidelines has the institution considered in developing the curricula of its various advanced programs?

G-1.5.2 What information shows that the guidelines identified in G-1.5.1 have been critically examined in relation to the planning and development of the advanced programs offered by the institution?

G-1.6 Quality Controls

The institution provides the faculty competence and the physical resources that are needed to support its graduate curricula. In addition, it creates conditions under which the graduate curricula can be effectively implemented. In the three standards which follow, certain quality controls are selected for fuller explication without presuming these controls to be the only important ones. They are the institution's policies for determining which courses and seminars are counted for graduate credit in programs of study, its policies for offering certain courses and seminars at the graduate level, and its requirements for full-time residence study.

G-1.6.1 Graduate Credit. Advanced programs require a level of study and performance beyond that required for the beginning professional. For this reason the institution establishes clear policies regarding work prerequisite to graduate credit for courses, seminars, readings, and/or other learning experiences which are included in students' programs of study.

Standard: *Institutional policies preclude the granting of graduate credit for study which is remedial or which is designed to remove deficiencies in meeting the requirements for admission to advanced programs.*

G-1.6.1a What regulations govern the granting of graduate credit in the advanced programs?

G-1.6.1b What evidence shows that the institution's regulations for granting graduate credit are enforced?

G-1.6.2 Graduate Level Courses. The character of advanced programs is influenced by the mature status and the professional motivation of graduate students. While there may be good reasons for admitting undergraduate students to some graduate courses, it is assumed that for substantial periods of time in advanced programs, students are in instructional groups in which only graduate students are enrolled.

Standard: *At least one-half of the requirements of curricula leading to a master's degree and to a sixth-year certificate or degree are met by courses, seminars, and other learning experiences offered only to graduate students; at least two-thirds of the requirements of curricula leading to the doctorate are met by courses, seminars, and other learning experiences offered only to graduate students.*

G-1.6.2a What is the institution's policy with regard to the proportion of undergraduate work that may be counted toward degrees or the proportion of graduate study that must be included in degree programs at each level (master's, sixth-year, doctoral)?

G-1.6.2b What evidence shows that the stated policy is enforced?

G-1.6.3 Residence Study. One of the desirable characteristics of advanced study is that students learn from each other and through close association with the faculty in a climate that stimulates research and scholarly effort. This is not possible unless the student spends a substantial block of time in full-time residence at the institution.

Standard: *Some period of full-time continuous residence study, or provision for comparable experiences is required for candidates pursuing advanced degree other than the doctorate; at least one academic year full-time continuous residence study is required f candidates pursuing the doctorate.*

G-1.6.3a What are the institution's requirements for full-time residence study for each degree (or certificate) program? What are the precise definitions of "full-time" and "residence"?

G-1.6.3b What evidence shows that the residence study requirement was met by those candidates who received the master's degree and the sixth-year certificate or degree during the past two years?

G-1.6.3c What evidence shows that the one-year, full-time residence study requirement was met by each candidate who received the doctorate during the past two years?

G-1.7 Control of Advanced Programs

The quality of the graduate programs depends on the quality of the faculty and students as well as on the content and design of the several curricula. It follows that the institution needs a structure by which the faculty can control every phase of the advanced programs. Procedures for admitting students, planning programs, adding new courses, hiring staff, and determining requirements for degrees are carefully organized and systematized, and faculty members are involved in the formation and execution of both policy and procedures.

Schools or departments of education are sometimes expected to provide training for teachers and other professional school personnel through courses, seminars, and workshops that are offered primarily at the convenience of school personnel in the field. Frequently this training is applied toward meeting the requirements of a graduate certificate or degree. The institution ensures that such courses, seminars, and workshops—regardless of the location and time at which the instruction takes place—are taught by qualified faculty members and supported by essential learning resources. In addition, the institution ensures that the requirements for earning credit are comparable to those made in regular graduate offerings.

Standard: *The primary responsibility for initiation, development, and implementation of advanced programs lies with the education faculty.*

G-1.7.1 What is the administrative structure for controlling the advanced programs and what is the supporting rationale?

G-1.7.2 How are advanced programs initiated? What bodies approve changes and new programs?

G-1.7.3 What activities of the education faculty demonstrate that they have assumed responsibility for the initiation, development, and approval of all advanced programs?

G-1.7.4 What information shows that the faculty controls the quality of all courses, seminars, and workshops offered primarily at the convenience of school personnel in the field (such as at off-campus locations and at "irregular" hours) and counted as credit toward graduate degrees or certificates?

G-2. Faculty for Advanced Programs

The specialized nature of the content of advanced programs requires faculty with a high degree of specialization and competence. The competence of faculty as evidenced by their formal preparation and by their commitment to scholarship, research, and professional practice is critical to the quality of instruction offered. The following standards deal with aspects of faculty competence in relation to the development, execution, and review of the advanced programs, and with conditions conducive to effective faculty performance. "Faculty for advanced programs" is defined to include those members of the faculty who carry responsibilities for instruction, advisement, supervision, and research in the graduate programs for the advanced preparation of teachers and for the preparation of other professional school personnel.

G-2.1 Preparation of Faculty

The academic preparation of faculty members is one indicator of their competence. It is assumed that the doctor's degree in a well-defined field of specialization, earned in a regionally-accredited institution or a recognized foreign institution, is the minimal requirement for offering graduate instruction in advanced programs. Exceptions to that principle are made only in unusual cases when the faculty member—by virtue of publication, research, or professional recognition—has demonstrated his competence for independent scholarly activity.

Competence of faculty members is also determined by their scholarly performance and their experience in professional practice. Faculty members are expected to display a high order of active scholarship and to have done original research and they should have appropriate experience in professional practice to support the respective advanced programs.

Standard: *Faculty members teaching at the master's level in advanced programs hold the doctorate with advanced study in each field of specialization in which they are teaching or have demonstrated competence in such fields; those teaching at the sixth-year and doctoral levels hold the doctorate with study in each field of specialization in which they are teaching and conducting research. Faculty members who conduct the advanced programs at all degree levels are engaged in scholarly activity that supports their fields of special-*

ization and have experience which relates directly to their respective fields.

    G-2.1.1 What evidence shows that each faculty member teaching at the master's level holds the doctorate from a regionally-accredited institution or a recognized foreign university with advanced study in each field of specialization in which he teaches, or has demonstrated competence in his field of specialization?

    G-2.1.2 What evidence shows that each faculty member teaching at the sixth-year and/or doctoral level holds the doctorate from a regionally-accredited institution or a recognized foreign university with study in each field of specialization in which he teaches and/or conducts research?

    G-2.1.3 What information shows that each faculty member who teaches and/or conducts research in the advanced programs has had field experiences during the past five years which support his teaching and research assignments?

    G-2.1.4 What data show that each faculty member who teaches in the advanced programs has been engaged during the past two years in writing, research, and/or consultation, and that these activities support his teaching assignment?

G-2.2 Composition of Faculty for Doctoral Degree Programs

The adequacy of faculty for advanced programs is determined not only by their academic preparation, experience, and scholarly performance, but also by the distribution of their specializations and by the number of faculty members available for the tasks to be done. This is so, particularly for faculty for doctoral programs. A doctoral program requires a faculty that includes specialists for each field of specialization, and in addition, at least three specialists in fields which directly support each degree program.

Standard: *The faculty for each advanced program leading to the doctorate includes at least one full-time person who holds the doctorate with specialization in the field in which the degree is offered, and at least three persons who hold the doctorate in fields which directly support each degree program.*

    G-2.2.1 What evidence shows that there is at least one full-time person who holds the doctorate with appropriate specialization for each advanced program in which the doctor's degree is offered?

    G-2.2.2 What data confirm that there are at least three specialists who hold doctorates in fields which directly support each degree program offered?

G-2.3 Conditions for Faculty Service

The faculty is the major determinant of the quality of advanced programs. Conditions that make possible a high level of performance include reasonable faculty load, adequate support for faculty research, opportunities for faculty development, and essential supporting services.

Faculty load policies give due consideration to the responsibilities assigned to a graduate faculty member, including the planning and teaching of courses and seminars, advisement of students, supervision of experiences in professional practice and of dissertations, research activities, participation in program development, and activities requisite to professional development. The policies establish a maximum limit for faculty teaching loads and this limit is lower than that established for the loads of undergraduate faculty. Furthermore, these policies take into account the special demands that are made on faculty who carry responsibilities for doctoral programs.

The institution provides time and some financial support to enable faculty members to engage in research. Faculty in advanced programs engage in research to contribute to the solution of educational problems, to expand the field of knowledge in education, and to provide a model for student learning.

To maintain and to improve the quality of its faculty, the institution has a plan for faculty development which provides such opportunities as in-service education, sabbatical leave, travel support, summer leaves, intra- and inter-institutional visitation, and fellowships. In addition, time is allocated in the load of a faculty member so that he can continue his scholarly development.

The institution recognizes that the quality of its instructional programs can be compromised if faculty members dissipate their energy in subprofessional tasks. Therefore, provision is made for supporting services (such as those provided by instructional media technicians, instructional assistants, research assistants, project assistants, secretaries, and clerks) that permit faculty members to fulfill their instructional, research, and other responsibilities at a high level of performance.

Standard: *The institution provides conditions essential to the effective performance by the faculty in the advanced programs.*

    G-2.3.1 What is the plan for taking into account a professional duties and activities of th faculty in determining load?

G-2.3.2 What has been the total load assigned to each faculty member in the advanced programs over all terms during the last two years and what are the duties (such as teaching courses, advising students, supervising experiences in professional practice, supervising or chairing dissertations, research, committee assignments, professional development, and others) that make up each load?

G-2.3.3 What is the institution's policy regarding the provision of time for faculty to engage in research, and what evidence shows that this policy is being implemented?

G-2.3.4 What evidence indicates that the institution provides financial support to encourage research activities by faculty in the advanced programs?

G-2.3.5 What is the institution's plan for the continuous professional development of faculty in the advanced programs and what evidence shows that it is operative?

G-2.3.6 What is the plan for allocating supporting services to faculty in the advanced programs and what evidence shows that such services are provided?

G-2.4 Part-Time Faculty

Successful professionals outside the institution often can add strength to advanced programs and frequently the demand for a particular course is too small to warrant the employment of a full-time faculty member. The standard does not specify an acceptable ratio of part-time to full-time faculty. However, in the interests of operating acceptable graduate programs, the institution prevents the fragmentation of instruction and the erosion of program quality that can accompany excessive use of part-time faculty.

Standard: *Part-time faculty meet the requirements for appointment to the full-time faculty and are employed only when they can make special contributions to advanced programs.*

G-2.4.1 What proportion of each advanced program is assigned to part-time faculty?

G-2.4.2 What evidence shows that each part-time faculty member meets the requirements for appointment to the full-time graduate faculty?

G-2.4.3 What reasons support the utilization of each part-time faculty member in the advanced programs?

G-3. Students in Advanced Programs

Graduate programs for the advanced preparation of teachers and for the preparation of other professional school personnel require students of promise and ability whose success in professional practice can be reasonably predicted. The quality of the advanced programs is significantly influenced by the quality of students admitted because of the greater dependence on self-instruction and individual scholarship required by study at the graduate level. Attention to the characteristics of students admitted to, retained in, and graduated from advanced programs is essential to designing and maintaining acceptable programs. It is assumed in the standards which follow that an institution applies criteria for admission to, and retention in, its advanced programs; provides for supervision of students' programs of study; provides opportunities for student participation in program evaluation and development; and that it evaluates graduates. The evaluation of graduates is treated in another section of the standards.

G-3.1 Admission to Advanced Programs

Students enter advanced programs at various points in their careers and with a variety of academic backgrounds. Moreover, different fields of specialization require different abilities: some are more theoretical than others; some place more emphasis on personal relations than do others. Thus, there can be no single set of admission requirements for all programs. The institution, nevertheless, establishes and applies a number of criteria for admitting students to each advanced program and to each program level (master's, sixth-year, doctoral). These criteria, both objective and subjective, reflect a rational process for selecting students whose success in the respective specialties can be reasonably predicted.

Standard: *The institution applies specific criteria for admission to each advanced program at each level; these criteria require the use of both objective and subjective data.*

G-3.1.1 What are the admission requirements for each advanced program and at each level (master's, sixth-year, doctoral)?

G-3.1.2 What evidence indicates that the institution's requirements for admission to advanced programs are being met?

G-3.1.3 What objective data, including test results with national norms, are used for admitting students to advanced programs?

G-3.1.4 What characteristics of the students admitted to advanced programs are revealed by the data obtained through applying objective and subjective criteria?

G-3.2 Retention of Students in Advanced Programs

The maintenance of acceptable advanced programs demands that the institution establish and apply criteria not only for the selection of students, but also for the continuous screening of those students who have been admitted. The profession requires that the practitioner demonstrate academic and technical competence as well as those personal characteristics which are appropriate to the requirements of the school position for which he is preparing.

Because the failing grade in graduate courses is rarely given, "satisfactory progress" frequently has to be judged by subjective criteria. However, subjective judgments are inadequate unless the institution first has ways of formally collecting and evaluating these judgments, and then of translating them into a decision on the student's status.

Standard: *The institution applies specific criteria for the retention of candidates in advanced programs who possess academic competencies and personal characteristics appropriate to the requirements of the professional roles for which they are being prepared.*

G-3.2.1 What is the plan and its supporting rationale for ensuring that only qualified candidates are permitted to continue in each advanced program and at each program level (master's, sixth-year, doctoral)?

G-3.2.2 How many students have not been permitted to continue in each advanced program during the past two years and for what reasons? Under what circumstances, if any, may such students reenter the advanced programs?

G-3.2.3 What is the average and the range for the length of time required which students took to complete master's programs during the past two years? Sixth-year programs? Doctoral programs?

G-3.3 Planning and Supervision of Students' Programs of Study

The same considerations that make admission to an advanced program a highly individualized matter also operate in the planning and supervision of each graduate student's program of study. Planning of each program of study is done jointly by the student concerned and an officially designated faculty advisor. Responsibility for sponsoring each thesis, dissertation, or field study is assigned to an official advisor who is a member of the faculty conducting the advanced programs and whose specialization is appropriate to the thesis, dissertation, or field study topic. It is assumed that both students and faculty members have a choice in the assignment of advisors. The intent of this standard is to prevent perfunctory program planning while protecting the flexibility needed for individualizing programs of study.

Standard: *The program of study for each student in the advanced programs is jointly planned by the student and a member of the faculty; the program of study for each doctoral candidate is approved by a faculty committee; the sponsorship of each thesis, dissertation, or field study is the responsibility of a member of the faculty with specialization in the area of the thesis, dissertation, or field study.*

G-3.3.1 What provisions ensure that each graduate student's program of study is jointly planned by the student and an official faculty advisor?

G-3.3.2 What evidence indicates that each doctoral candidate's program of study is approved by a faculty committee?

G-3.3.3 What evidence shows that the sponsorship of each thesis, dissertation, or field study (master's, sixth-year, doctoral) is assigned to a qualified member of the faculty?

G-3.3.4 What information indicates that both students and faculty members have a choice in the assignment of advisors?

G-3.4 Student Participation in Program Evaluation and Development

As members of the higher education community, graduate students in the advanced programs have the opportunity and responsibility to express their views regarding the improvement of the respective preparation programs in which they are enrolled. Through student organizations, through joint student-faculty groups, and/or through membership on faculty committees, students have clear channels and frequent opportunities to express their views with the assurance that their proposals will influence the development of the advanced programs offered by the institution.

Standard: *The institution has representative student participation in the evaluation and development of its advanced programs.*

G-3.4.1 What evidence shows that graduate students participate in the evaluation and development of advanced programs?

G-3.4.2 What are the major concerns which students have expressed during the last two years and in what ways have these concerns influenced the development of advanced programs?

G-4. Resources and Facilities for Advanced Programs

The institution provides resources and physical facilities which support the advanced programs it offers The adequacy of these resources and facilities i systematically evaluated in relation to the demands made upon them by advanced curricula, faculty, and students.

Advanced programs make greater demands on institutional resources than do undergraduate programs. This is especially so for doctoral programs. Institutions offering or proposing to offer advanced programs should demonstrate that the resources are available for these programs and without their impairing the quality of the undergraduate programs in the same institution.

G-4.1 Library

The adequacy of library holdings is a major factor in establishing the quality of advanced programs. As the principal educational materials resource and the information storage and retrieval center of an institution, the library holdings are adequate for the number of students and faculty to be served, and pertinent to the kind and level of graduate programs offered. The operation of advanced programs requires library resources substantially larger than those required for basic programs. The library resources required for doctoral programs vary widely but, in any case, they are substantial, and considerably exceed those for master's programs.

The recommendations of faculty members and professional organizations are given serious consideration in maintaining and building the collection. Adequate library service is provided to assure that students and faculty members have access to the holdings.

Standard: *The library provides resources that are adequate to support instruction, independent study, and research required for each advanced program.*

G-4.1.1 What evidence indicates that the library collection includes standard and contemporary holdings (books, microfilms, microfiche copies, periodicals) to support each advanced program?

G-4.1.2 What information shows that the institution, in maintaining and improving the quality of its library holdings, gives serious considera- to the recommendations of:
  a. Faculty members?
  b. Appropriate national professional organizations and learned societies?
  c. A nationally recognized list (or lists) of books and periodicals?

G-4.1.3 What information indicates that students in advanced programs have access to, and use, the library holdings?

G-4.1.4 What is the annual record of library expenditures for the total library and for the advanced programs during the past five years?

G-4.2 Physical Facilities and Other Resources

Advanced programs draw on the full range of institutional resources to support instruction and research. The extent to which physical facilities, equipment, and specialized resources are required for graduate study depends on the particular program. It is assumed that such facilities and resources are readily accessible so that faculty and students may effectively pursue instructional objectives.

Standard: *The institution provides physical facilities and other resources essential to the instructional and research activities of each advanced program.*

G-4.2.1 What information confirms that faculty and students have instructional, research, and office space necessary to carry out their responsibilities?

G-4.2.2 What evidence shows that specialized equipment (such as open and closed television, computers) and laboratories necessary to support each advanced program are available, and that they are used by faculty and students?

G-4.2.3 What information indicates that the institution draws on the full range of its resources to support its advanced programs?

G-4.2.4 What information shows that the institution has given serious consideration to the recommendations of faculty members for improving physical facilities and other supporting resources?

G-5. Evaluation, Program Review, and Planning

Maintenance of acceptable programs for the advanced preparation of teachers and for the preparation of other professional school personnel requires the systematic evaluation of the quality of the professionals who complete the programs, modification of existing programs, and long-range planning. It is recognized that the relationship between effectiveness of preparation and quality of effort in the profession may be difficult to assess; but without continuing and conscientious effort, planning for and making improvements have little solid basis. The development of effective processes for evaluation, the impact of the evaluation results on the curricula of the advanced programs and systematic planning for the future are all critical elements for assessing the quality of advanced programs in terms of the objectives sought. Accordingly, the institution engages in the continuous review of program objectives through the interrelation of the curricula, faculty, students, and the resources available for the tasks.

G-5.1 Evaluation of Graduates

Criteria for admission to, and retention in, advanced programs provide some assurance that students of promise and ability enter and continue in programs offered, but such criteria do not ensure that candidates of promise and ability will complete the programs, nor that they will enter school positions for which they have been prepared, nor that they will perform satisfactorily after assuming their professional roles. The ultimate criterion for judging advanced programs is whether they produce graduates who enter the profession and perform effectively. The institution evaluates its graduates at two critical points: when they complete their programs of study, and after they enter the professional roles for which they have prepared.

It is recognized that the means now available for making such evaluations are not fully adequate. Nevertheless, the standard assumes that an institution evaluates the school personnel it prepares with the best means now available, and that it attempts to develop improved means for making such evaluations. As progress is made toward more adequate evaluation procedures, this standard will become increasingly important.

Any effort to assess the quality of graduates requires that evaluations be made in relation to the objectives sought. Therefore, an institution uses the stated objectives of a particular advanced program as a basis for evaluating the graduates of that program.

Standard: *The institution conducts a well-defined plan for evaluating the teachers and other professional school personnel it prepares at the graduate level.*

G-5.1.1 What information shows that the stated objectives for each advanced program are used as a basis for evaluating the graduates of the respective programs?

G-5.1.2 What means are used to collect data about teachers and other professional school personnel prepared in the advanced programs:
a. At the point of program completion?
b. After they enter the professional roles for which they are prepared?

G-5.1.3 What information shows that the institution is keeping abreast of new developments in the evaluation of graduates and is engaged in efforts to improve its plan for making such evaluations?

G-5.1.4 What percent of the teachers and other professional school personnel prepared at the graduate level during the last two years actually entered the professional roles for which they prepared?

G-5.1.5 What characteristics of school personnel prepared in the advanced programs have been revealed through evaluation of graduates?

G-5.2 Use of Evaluation Results to Improve Advanced Programs

The institution evaluates the teachers and other professional school personnel it prepares not only to obtain assessments of their quality, but also to provide information which identifies areas in the advanced programs that need strengthening and information which suggests new directions for program development. It is assumed that the results of the evaluations made by the institution are reflected in modifications in the preparation programs.

Standard: *The institution uses the evaluation results in the study, development, and improvement of its advanced programs.*

G-5.2.1 What strengths and weaknesses in the advanced programs have been revealed through evaluation of graduates?

G-5.2.2 What does the institution do to ensure that the results obtained from evaluating its graduates are translated into appropriate program modifications?

G-5.3 Long-Range Planning

Institutional plans for future development provide a basis for making decisions in such matters as increasing or limiting enrollment, expanding and/or upgrading present programs, discontinuing programs, or introducing new programs. Effective long-range planning presupposes that an institution periodically reevaluates program objectives in relation to societal changes, and that it engages in study and research to ascertain whether its present policies and practices are an effective means for accomplishing its purposes. It is assumed that the institutional community participates in conducting such studies and in projecting the long-run plans for advanced programs.

Standard: *The institution has plans for the long-range development of its advanced programs; these plans are part of a design for total institutional development.*

G-5.3.1 What evidence indicates that the institution has, or is, engaged in studies and/or institutional research to improve its advanced programs?

G-5.3.2 What information shows that the faculty members conducting the advanced programs participate in the formulation of the institution's plans for the long-range development of these programs?

G-5.3.3 What is the institution's plan for future development of advanced programs and what rationale supports significant changes that are proposed?